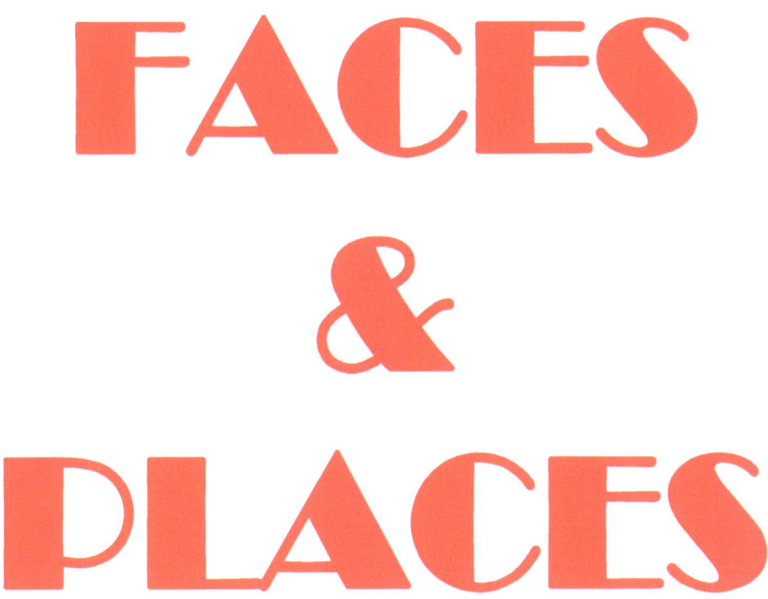

FACES & PLACES

Judith A. Gavin-Holton

DEDICATION

This is my first attempt at completing a book of art-work and dedicating it to my sister Patricia Marie, to my brother "Buddy" Arthur J. and my step-sister Kathy. To all my nieces, nephews, great nieces and great nephews who are forever remembered. May they always enjoy life, peace, health and love!

ACKNOWLEDGEMENTS

The Art work on the cover of this book represents a wonderful and enjoyable task given to me by my adult-childhood best friend, Bonnie L. Sprung Katzev, who sent me a paperback on how to play by doodling. Thus, I was able to *Ink-doodle* countless faces without connecting any of the lines. Editing done by: M.J. Mott and Mary D. Scott. This total package was put together with much care and expertise by my best friend Mary D. Scott. Warm, peaceful wishes and much gratitude to all, as their future journeys continue to bring them the best.

AUTHOR'S NOTE

I was 26 years of age in 1966, when registered nurse friends from Cedars Sinai Hospital invited me to fly with them to Europe for a *three-month travel around* to see various art museums such as the Louvre Museum in France, Michelangelo's Sistine Chapel in Italy and several of his finer works displayed throughout. This was a life changing opportunity to see real art completed by the original Artist. The Louvre took several days while we toured the city and neighboring towns. In England we visited Shakespeare's township and slept in the first of many Bed and Breakfast Inns.

While walking and sightseeing we came upon several people who were caught up in their own worlds and concerns. I saw their expressions and wanted very much to capture such. Using a camera would have changed all of that. So I decided to sketch what I placed to memory later in the day. Forty-seven years later, 2013, I discovered my little art pad hiding in an old suitcase pocket and decided to bring them to life using ink on 9" x 12" sketch pad. Then, in 2015, I decided to make them into a published art book.

The entire trip was centered on *Art*, a variety of cultures, International foods, Bed and Breakfast Inn surprises, socialization with those from other countries, and visiting with friends. Yes! I would do this again in a heartbeat.

TABLE OF CONTENTS

Chapter 1 - A KITTY A CANE AND A SACK

This young man while he appears to be a sleeping traveler-beggar with the ultimate hole in his left shoe is actually feeling the riches of the noon sunlight bouncing off the stain glass within the sanctuary of the building that bears a cross overhead. He has a peaceful sleeping kitty by his side, a cane to hold him up as if to be awake, his only belongings in a cloth sack, and a church cot to rest upon from his countless daily travels.

He is trusting in this unique surrounding that delivers much warmth, comfort, and serenity that affords him a much needed rest. A respite, which allows him the sanctuary of closing his eyes and drift off into a dream journey.

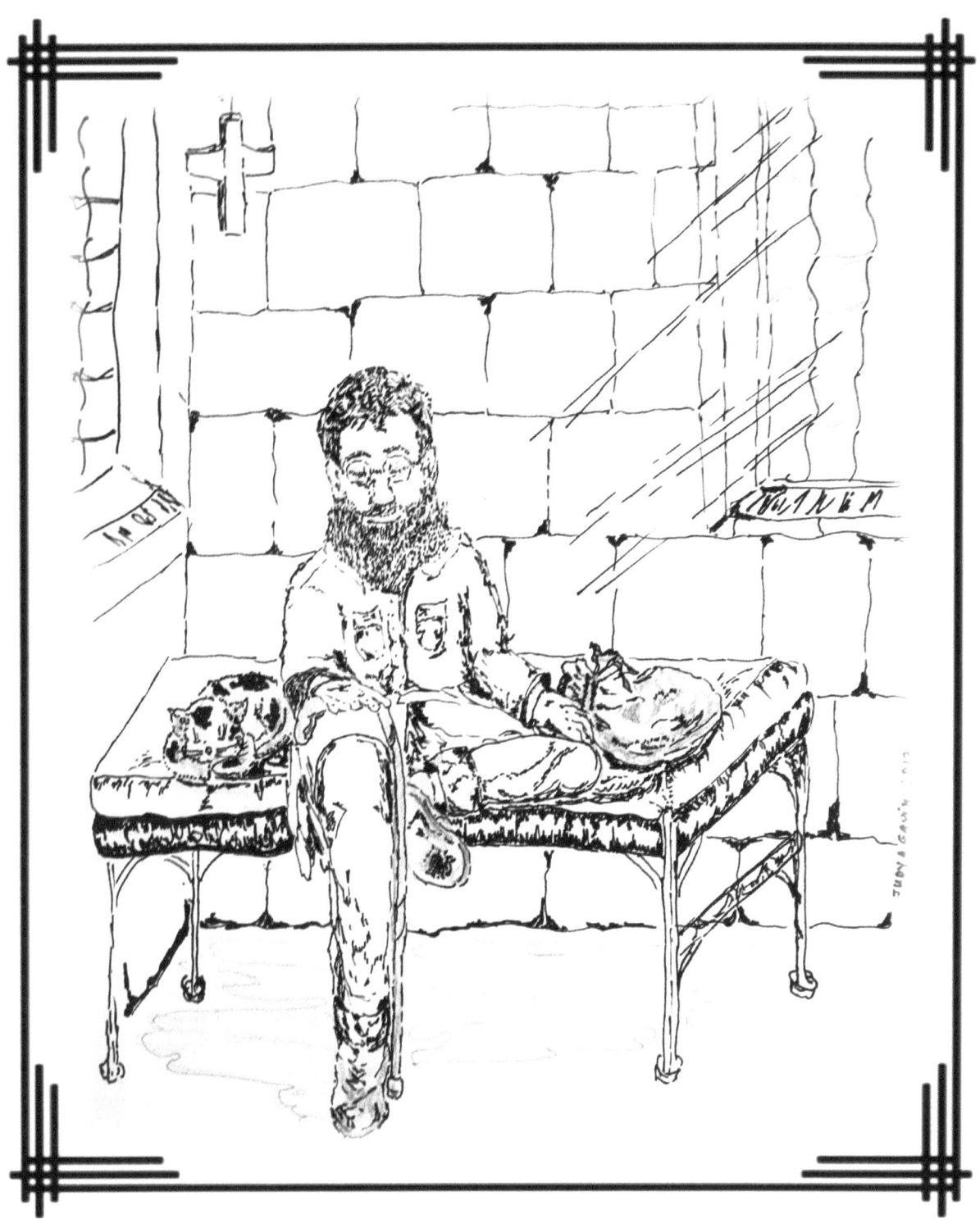

Sketched By: Judith A Gavin Holton, 2013
Small sketch done while in London, England, 1966

Chapter 2 – SAIL BOAT REPAIR

An older man seemed to be caught up with helping the young boy with his sailboat strings needing restoration. The young boy seemed saddened and frustrated just as much as the man trying to help. The boy appears to feel pain over the sails being broken and can't take his eyes off the man's fingers as they rework the new string. This was a small circular pond or pool in Paris, France, of less than three feet deep for small boat play-sailing by anyone who chose to. It was summer and other children were already playing while this poor chap could only hold his boat and ponder the same.

The man was quite intense as he carefully weaved the string to their rightful places in daunting silence. I sketched this on my tiny pad because I was in awe that each only saw the sails, the string and the boat.

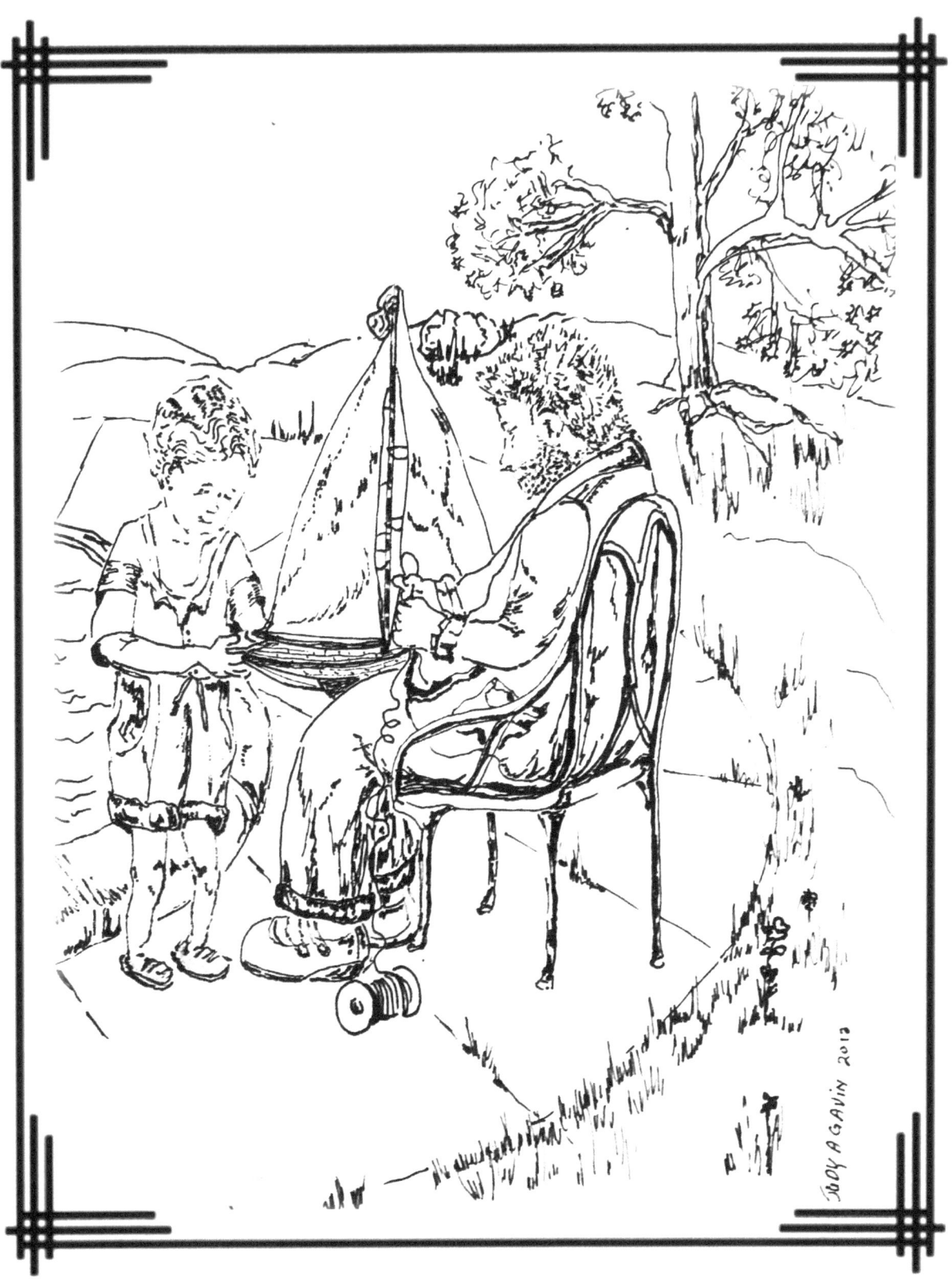

Sketched By: Judith A. Gavin-Holton, 2013
Small sketch done while in Paris, France, 1966

Chapter 3 – POLITENESS

This was the summer of 1966 and we were in Rome, Italy. I was one of four nurses on holiday from America and we stopped to get some fluids at an outside café. We had just finished walking through three art museums and it was quite warm…at least 101 degrees. Where we stopped a guitarist was playing soft melodies and seemingly to be enjoying his own music world. He sat on an upside down container and had a small three legged table off to his right for his monetary collection plate.

We were so appreciative of the calming melodies he produced that we placed American one dollar bills into his plate. Suddenly, he stopped playing and looked astonished by this unexpected gift from each of us. His face captured my thoughts and once again I sketched on my little art pad.

He smiled and strummed louder, then stood up with a complimentary smile and a bow. This we really enjoyed and stayed awhile.

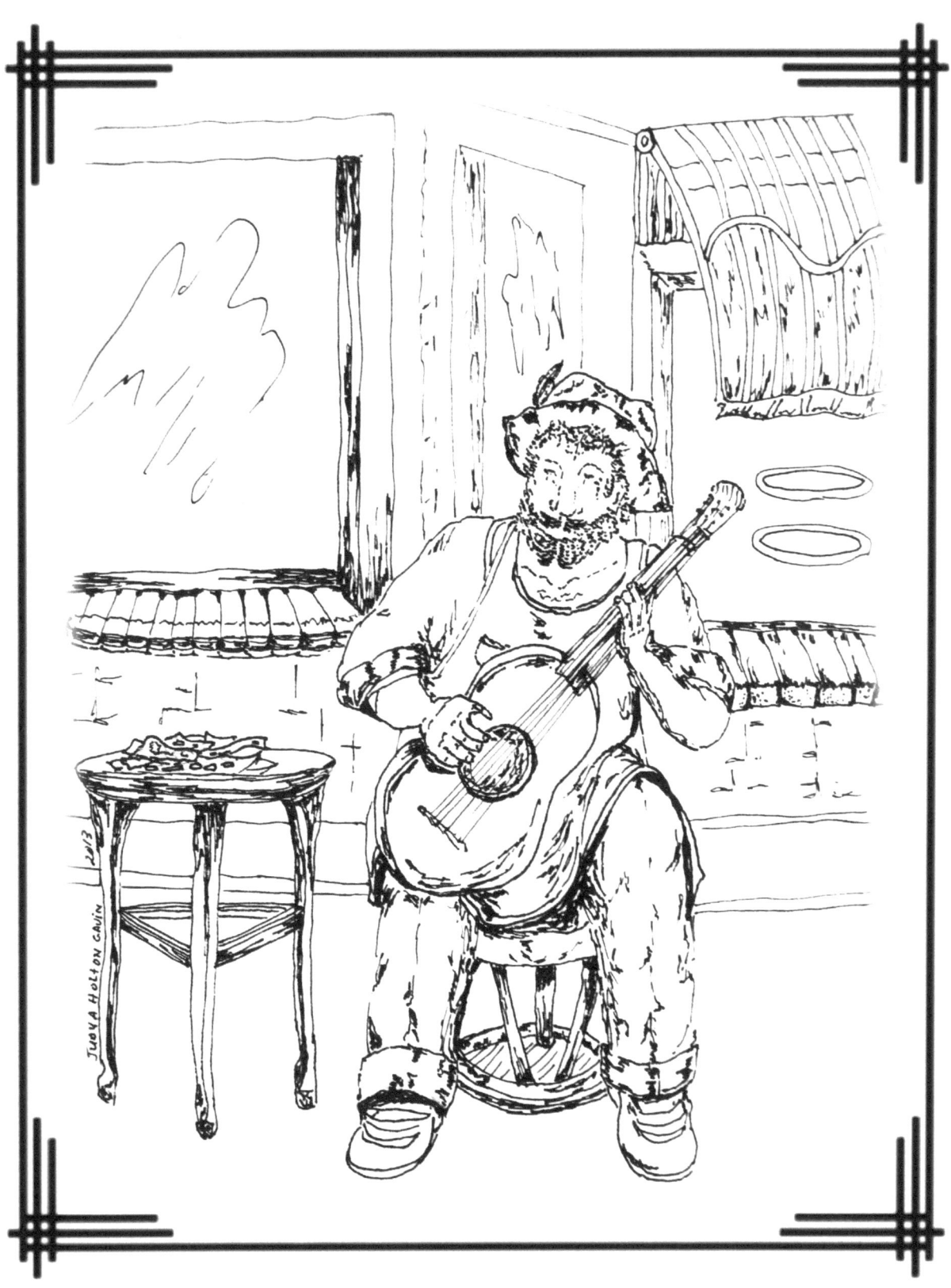

Sketched By: Judith A. Gavin-Holton, 2013
Small sketch done while in Rome, Italy, 1966

Chapter 4 – THE LITTLE RED CROSS DOLL

While in London, England my nurse friends and I noticed how high many of the "curbs" were. Some curbs were almost a foot high. The time was early morning in 1966 and we were walking around Piccadilly Square. I believe it was our third day in this lovely country. Across the street near where we were staying was this woman with a little girl sitting on her lap as if they were calmly waiting for someone. They wore a dark blue cloth folded in a triangle to hold their hair in place and had three satchels or one may have been her purse.

What caught my attention was the doll having a Red Cross on a nurse's cap. The doll also wore a white apron with a bib and it had a smaller Red Cross on it. So I sketched this scene including the high curb in my little pad. Using a camera would have spoiled the moment and photos make people uneasy when you don't know one another. Cameras in 1966 were not digital and it took time to manipulate a photo shoot.

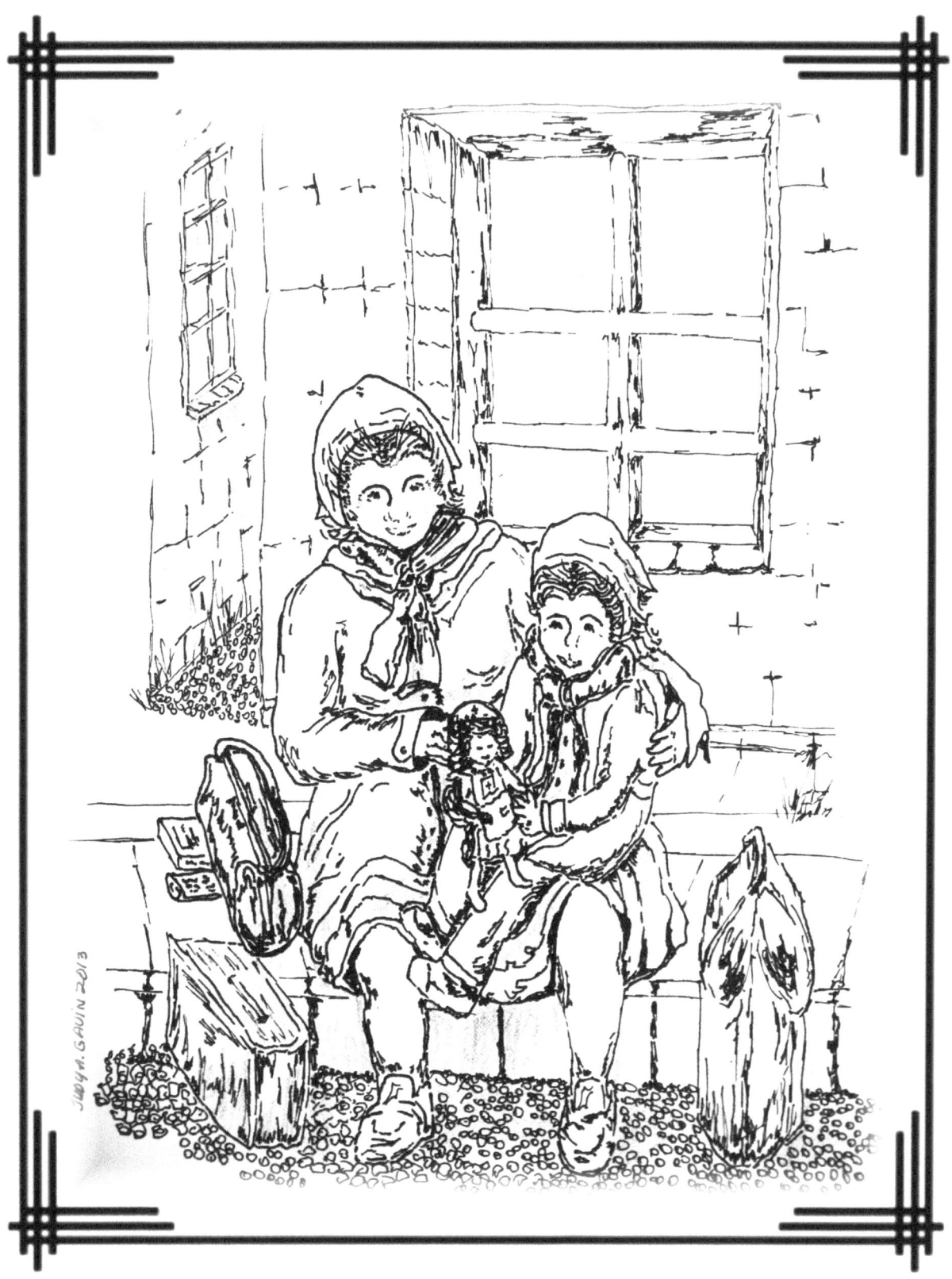

Sketched By: Judith A. Gavin-Holton, 2013
Small sketch done while in London, England, 1966

Chapter 5 – ALMOST A REAL MONKEY

This young man told us he was working his way through an English college for engineering and hoped one day to be an Engineer/Architect. He had built his music grinder machine from scratch. He used a post attached center below it whereby he could hold it up by stepping on a bracket attached at the bottom at the same time his left hand could turn the grinder handle thus provide music.

He made his little Monkey Puppet using a real cup for people to donate into. He couldn't afford a real-live monkey so he made a wooden one and dressed it. He had even sewn the blue and red outfit for the monkey and had made two more totally different changes. A wooden crate was used below the puppet to keep him clean while he made it dance.

The curb's height is representative of the many normal curbs seen in London, England. The Monkey Puppet could tip his hat, bow and dance and of course hold out his money cup. This fellow would also tell jokes and was a very pleasant gentleman.

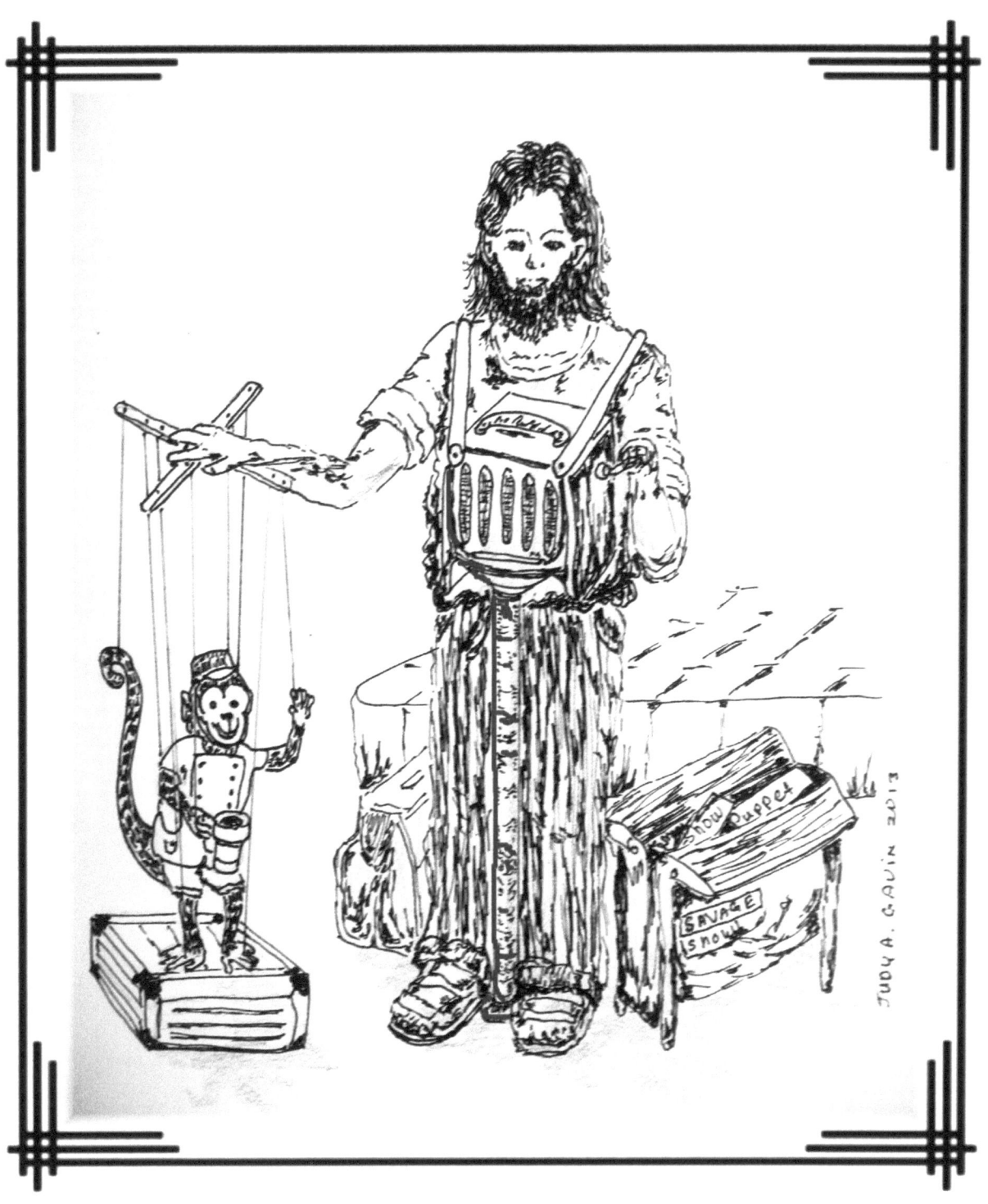

Sketched By: Judith A. Gavin-Holton, 2013
Small sketch done while in London, England, 1966

11

Chapter 6 – DRESS UP IN STYLE

A friend of mine came to Sun City's TEA PARTY wearing this gorgeous *BURGUNDY HAT* with several black feathery-plumes mixed with dark green leaves and two large very dark red roses at the top. She also wore a short-wasted jacket with scattered flowers in tandem to the hat. Around her neck was an antique brooch. On both her hands were partial fingerless black lace gloves from the 1920-1930s. In her hand of course was an original old English Tea cup and saucer. "Very regal she was."

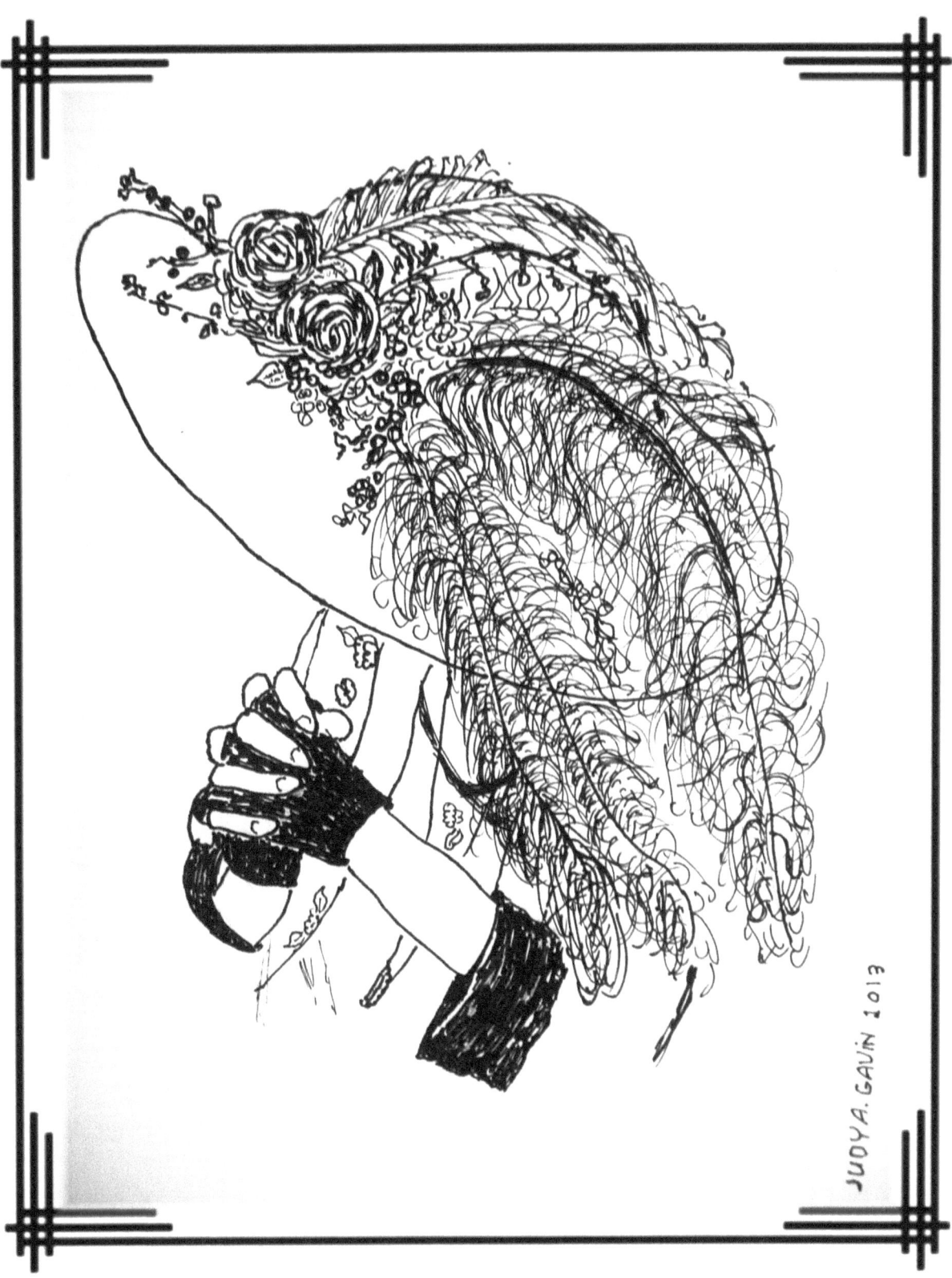

Sketched By: Judith A. Gavin-Holton [late summer] 2014

Chapter 7 – WHAT WAS YOUR FAVORITE DOLL?

I was waiting for the 3:16 p.m. bus to arrive with still fourteen minutes to go when a tiny lady appeared, standing behind me to my left.

She apparently was going to wait for the bus too. She stepped forward—within my peripheral vision—and started to talk. I gazed at her, saying nothing as she began her monologue. "Life, itself, is the journey we all take over and over," she said. "Each journey we take is about giving and taking from the depth of *inner souls*."

I looked around in every direction to see who she was talking to, only to find no one else was in sight. As she stepped next to me she asked a strange question.

"What was your favorite doll as a child?"

I felt strangely compelled to tell her without hesitation. At first I wondered, how could she know of the emotional pain and mental anguish I had once felt unless I did tell her? How could something from over sixty years ago still be so tender in thought? Had I repressed the hurting?

Later, I regretted that I had not even asked her why she wanted to know. But, that day, I just sat down on the bench to be at a level where I could look her in the eye and launched into my dolly story, first telling her where I had lived.

"As for my favorite doll, well, I had only one," I began. "I was about three and a half years old and lived at 165 Chester Street in Buffalo, New York." It was nearing noon; my brother Buddy and I were playing outside on a very cloudy, humid summer day. Even the birds seemed to be sweating because they were not singing. Mom called us in because it suddenly started to rain quite heavily, the large drops coming down in what people called a downpour.

We both were soaking wet within seconds and ran to get inside while Mom watched us. As the back door slammed shut with a *bang*, I began to quiver all over. I immediately remembered I had left my pretty dolly lying outside on the ground by my left side. I had placed her next to me while I dug into the dirt with an old tablespoon in my right hand. The rain had come down so hard and fast that I was getting drenched as I ran for cover carrying only the tablespoon. Inside, I suddenly stopped moving and started to cry uncontrollably. I told Mom I had left my dolly outside and wanted to go get her "NOW!" Even though she listened to me explain that my dolly was getting soaked, she was extremely firm and said "no" several times in a loud piercing voice. Tears, sniffles and begging meant nothing. My dolly was going to drown and die. I just knew it!

Still sobbing I decided to look outside for her and climbed up on the davenport. I crawled up to the pillows next to the two side windows off our small dining room, and 'sat ever so miserably sad' with my hands holding my head with my chin, to watch the utter demise of my one and only doll.

The rain beat like drums on the window pane. It kept rolling down just like my tears. I was crying the entire time, so hard were my tears that I wasn't sure if the rain was really getting me wet too. My face, hands, arms and shirt were covered with water. But, I continued to watch in absolute disbelief as the downpour not only soaked my doll's body but matted her cotton dress, her stuffed legs, her hair and her face. The deluge started to wash the pink soft rouge first from her skin on her cheeks, then her neck, and then her forehead. As her face disintegrated I could see the wires that were inside her head around her eyes. I did not know wires assisted her blue eyes to open and close as I changed her position while in my arms. When lying flat, her eyes closed and opened when I would pick her up.

Suddenly, without warning, as she lay there totally rainwater soaked, her eyes popped up to a stay open position. She looked directly at me with a frantic stare, as if I had killed her. I now cried even harder, asking my Mommy if I could get her before she died.

"Please, oh please let me go outside and get her," I pleaded. I even asked if my brother could go and retrieve her. "NO!" was shouted back at me.

I just knew I could dry her off and fix her. I could make new clothes for her.

"Please oh…Please," I begged. "Help me to save my Dolly."

"Mother did not even look out the window to see my *dying doll*." Not once.

So I watched till the very *end came* with those blue staring eyes watching me. All her skin slid away from her face, feet and hands revealing several mucky, beige glop-goo. As I watched, the rest of her body turned into a pile of matted dark gray cotton. The eye wires quite visible now. My heart sank into an abyss and I felt as though someone had stabbed me with a grubby nasty knife. I sat for a long time in wordless sorrow.

"Sleep didn't come easily. I cried myself to sleep that night. The hurt in my three year old heart was so intense that I made a conscious decision that I never wanted to feel that searing pain again. From that time on, I decided not to have nor own anything. I didn't realize at that age what it meant, but I became emotionally withdrawn and introverted. I was determined never to feel the powerful pain of loss again. All I could think was, she is gone now— my dolly was all gone—and I was sure I had killed her."

I paused to see if the tiny lady was still listening. She was and I continued.

"The next day I went outside and collected what was left of my dolly's remains and tried to bury her properly with my tablespoon in the side yard garden. But Mom took her fragile body from me to the garbage can, popped the metal lid and quickly dumped her improperly never saying a word. I had never prayed before but I tried saying simple three-year old words in forgiveness for my intense guilt."

"Later I told my Mom, I would never play dolls again and that she should *NOT EVER BUY ONE FOR ME* ever again! But she wasn't really listening."

"I was given many dolls, including an original red clothed Raggedy Anne & Andy dolls that today are worth quite a pretty penny. I never, never again played with any of the dolls. I just placed each doll given to me very neatly on my bed still in their wrappings. I kept all the dolls on my bed as ornaments because they weren't really mine. If they aren't mine then nothing bad can happen to them thus no heart sickening pain."

This tiny lady listened wordlessly, not missing a beat. I continued, "Sometime after I completed nursing school and had moved on with my life, I discovered that my mother had given all my 'Dolls, My Ornaments' to my brother's daughter for her future children. She still has them either wrapped or under glass because they were in exceptional condition and now invaluable."

The tiny lady I was talking to at the bus stop handed me a hankie. I hadn't felt any tears but she must have noticed them. I could tell she was astutely listening because her piercing blue eyes seemed to penetrate into the soul of my essence, as she listened to my journey.

Turning to look at her after I had finished the answer to her unique question, I said to her, "So when asked if I ever had a 'doll', I did, but she died when I was three and a half years old years old." The lady looked up at me with cheerfulness and a wonderful gentle smile. The tiny lady said, "Your dolly never died. She will continue to live forever in your heart and follow your inspiring journeys."

By this time I was wiping a few hidden tears that had rolled down my cheeks away with the hankie when the bus came. I stood up and turned to let the kind tiny lady board the bus first. But I saw no one as I turned completely around. When the bus doors opened I asked the bus driver if he saw which direction the little lady had gone, but he said I was alone as he approached the bus stop.

As I entered the stairway, the driver answered again saying, "I saw no one but you miss."

I was quite dumbfounded and wanted to go look for her to thank her but the driver said it was, "time to move on." So I boarded the bus and I never saw her again. The hankie, as I began to refold it, had the tiny blue letters *D.O.L.L.Y.* embroidered in the curve of the final corner. I smiled for weeks after knowing it was a real journey of life with serene heartfelt peace. I realized too that I had experienced a real life journey into emotional harmony.

Being able to write this narrative has helped me to understand—the way it was in 1943—my deliverance from self guilt and penalty pain to have become a lifelong humble caring human being as an adult.

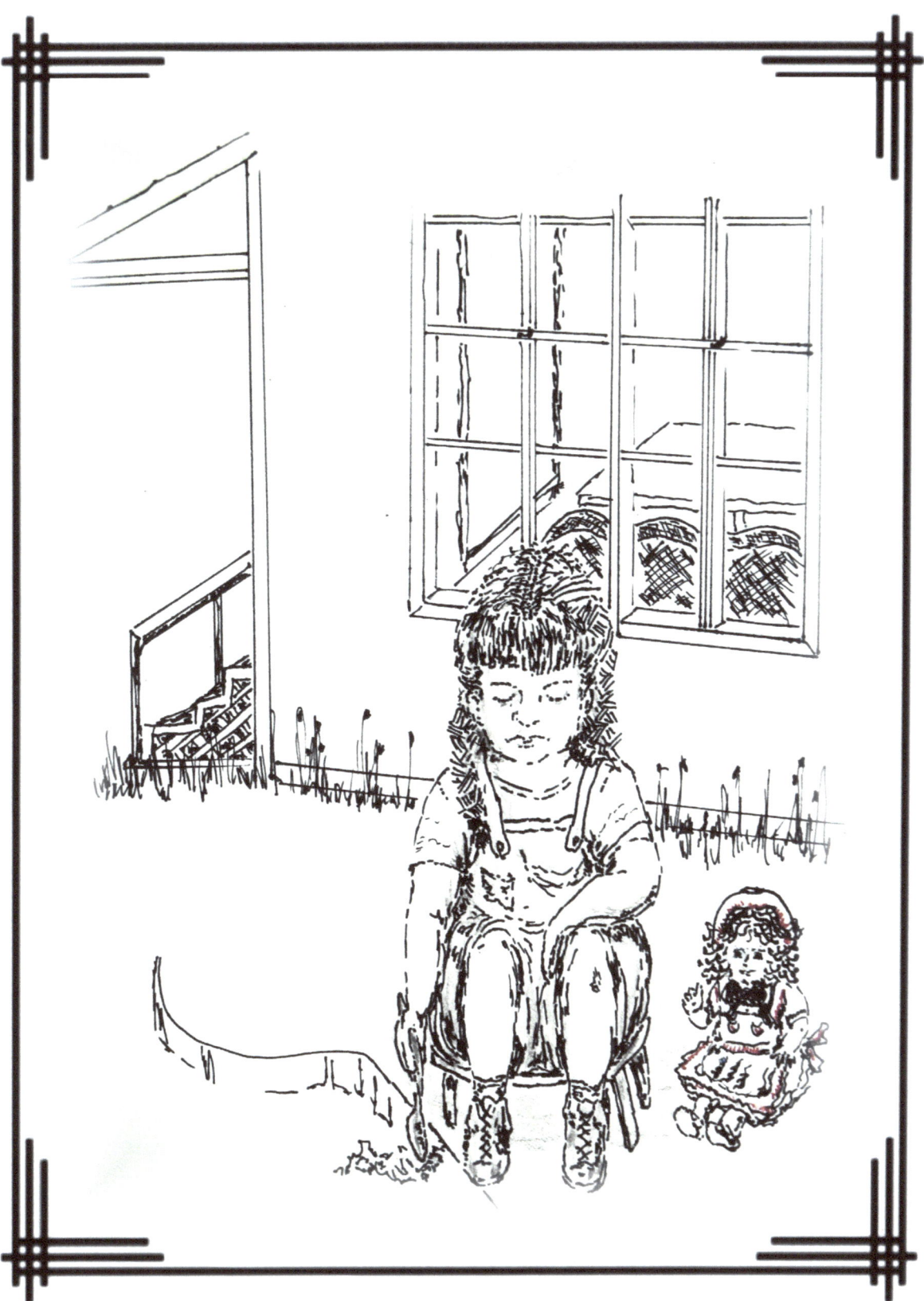

Sketched By: Judith A. Gavin-Holton [late summer] 2014

Chapter 8 – ENGLAND 1966 BUS STOP

This grand lady was going or coming from a trip during the summer rains with her family. The children may be her niece and nephew or her grandchildren. She had her arms stretched out wrapping them with loving care.

She wears a veil over her face as many folks did in this era for church services or special family visits. The children were wearing rain jackets with hoods and galoshes. They were staying close to her as if a tender call for the heart. They were the only ones at the bus stop when I made a mental picture and later sketched a little 3"x5" picture hours later.

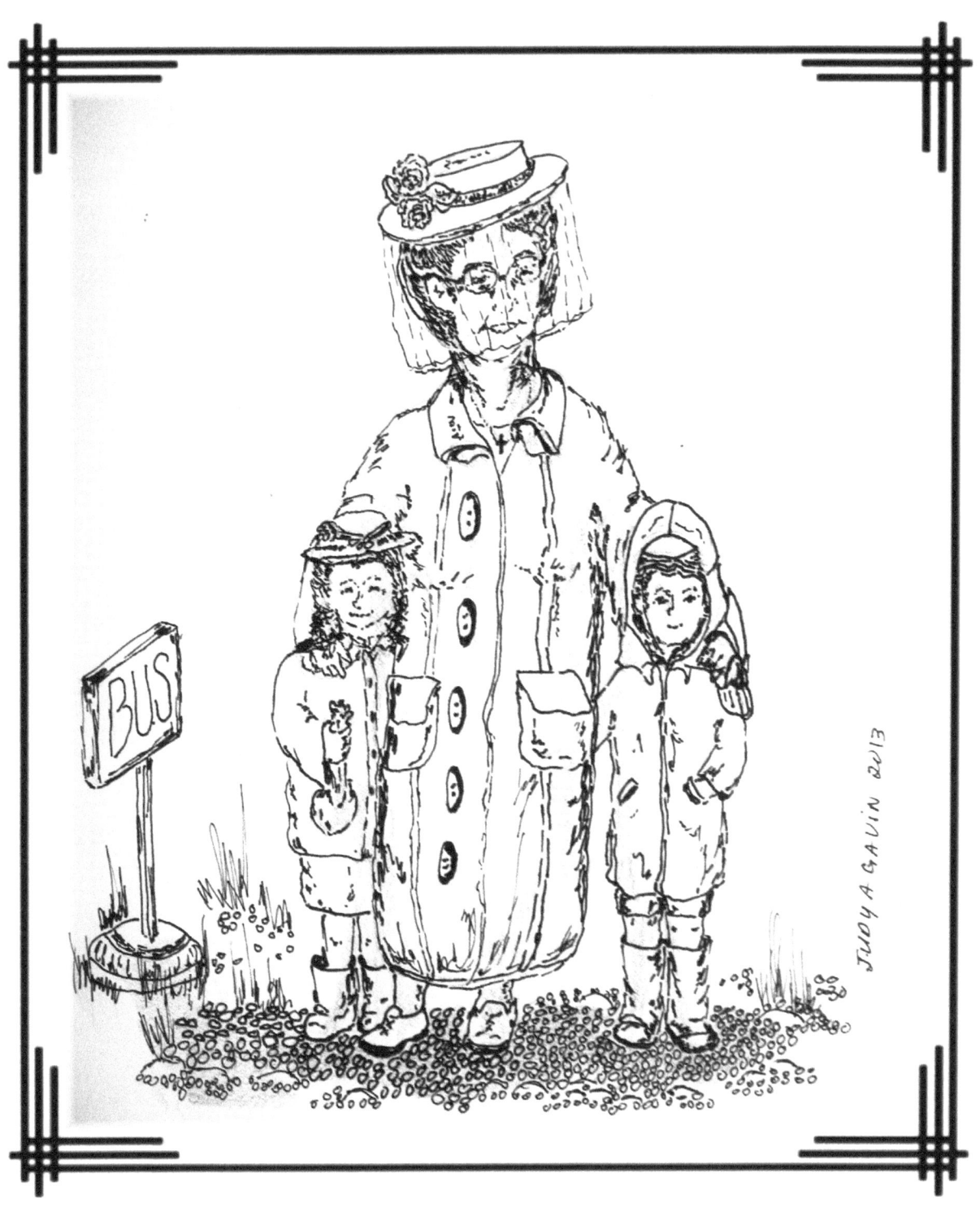

Sketched By: Judith A. Gavin-Holton [late summer] 2013
Small sketch done while in London, England, 1966

Chapter 9 – NOTES AND MORE NOTES

A young lady is using a pen, paper and an iPad to help her with utmost note taking. She is sitting in attendance outside of a kitchen counter on a spin-counter-stool and her sleeves are rolled up in preparation for wisdom enhancements. I made mental-camera notes and then ink-sketched them much later.

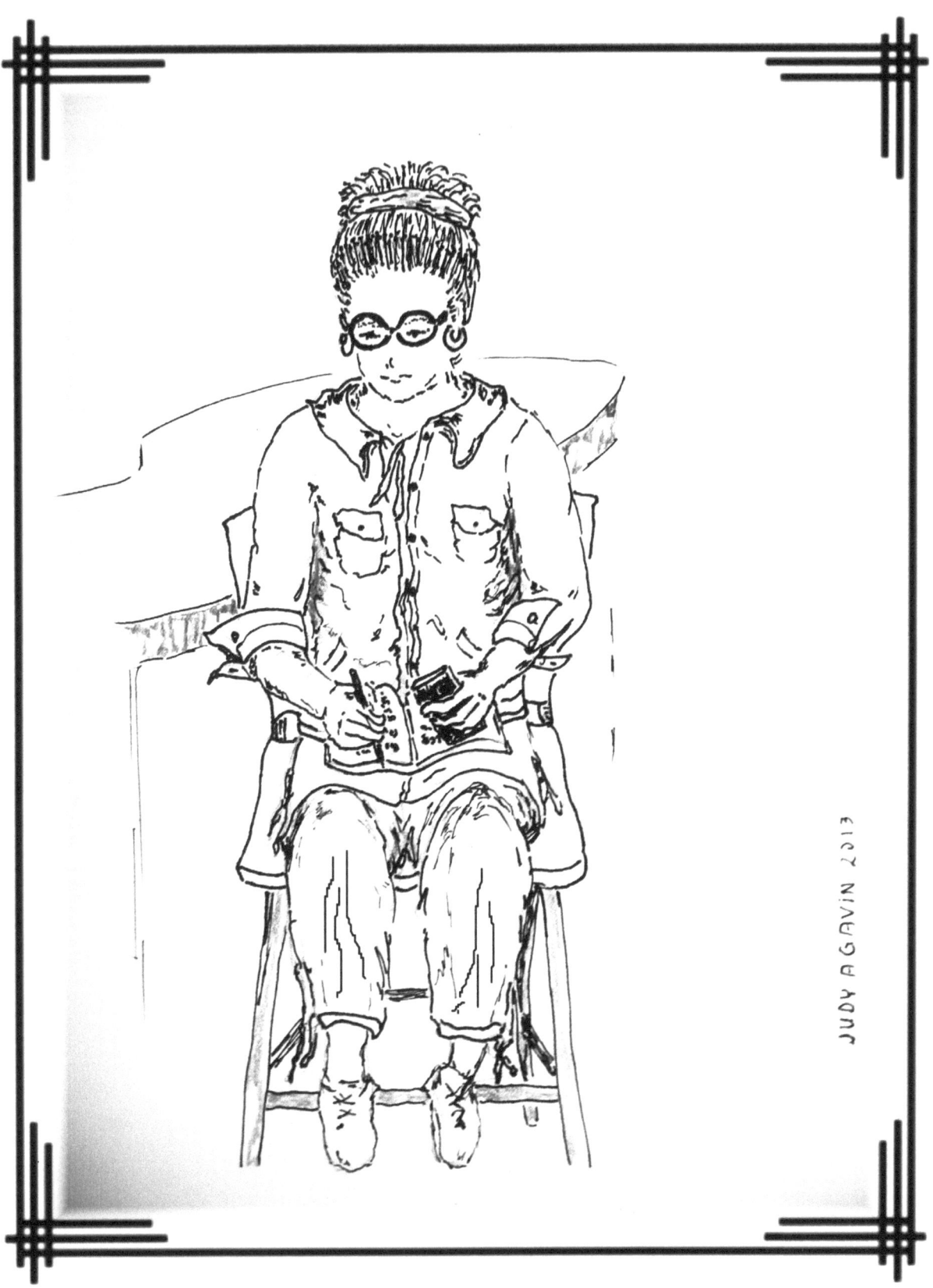

Sketched By: Judith A. Gavin-Holton [late summer] 2014

23

Chapter 10 – MUSIC TO ENJOY A MEAL WITH

Several friends visited Old Town San Diego for lunch and had a real live treat with these two gentlemen playing their guitars as they walked around. One wore a hat while the other did not. They played and smiled and nodded to the appreciative clapping hands. It was a beautiful afternoon and the folks all seemed cheerful.

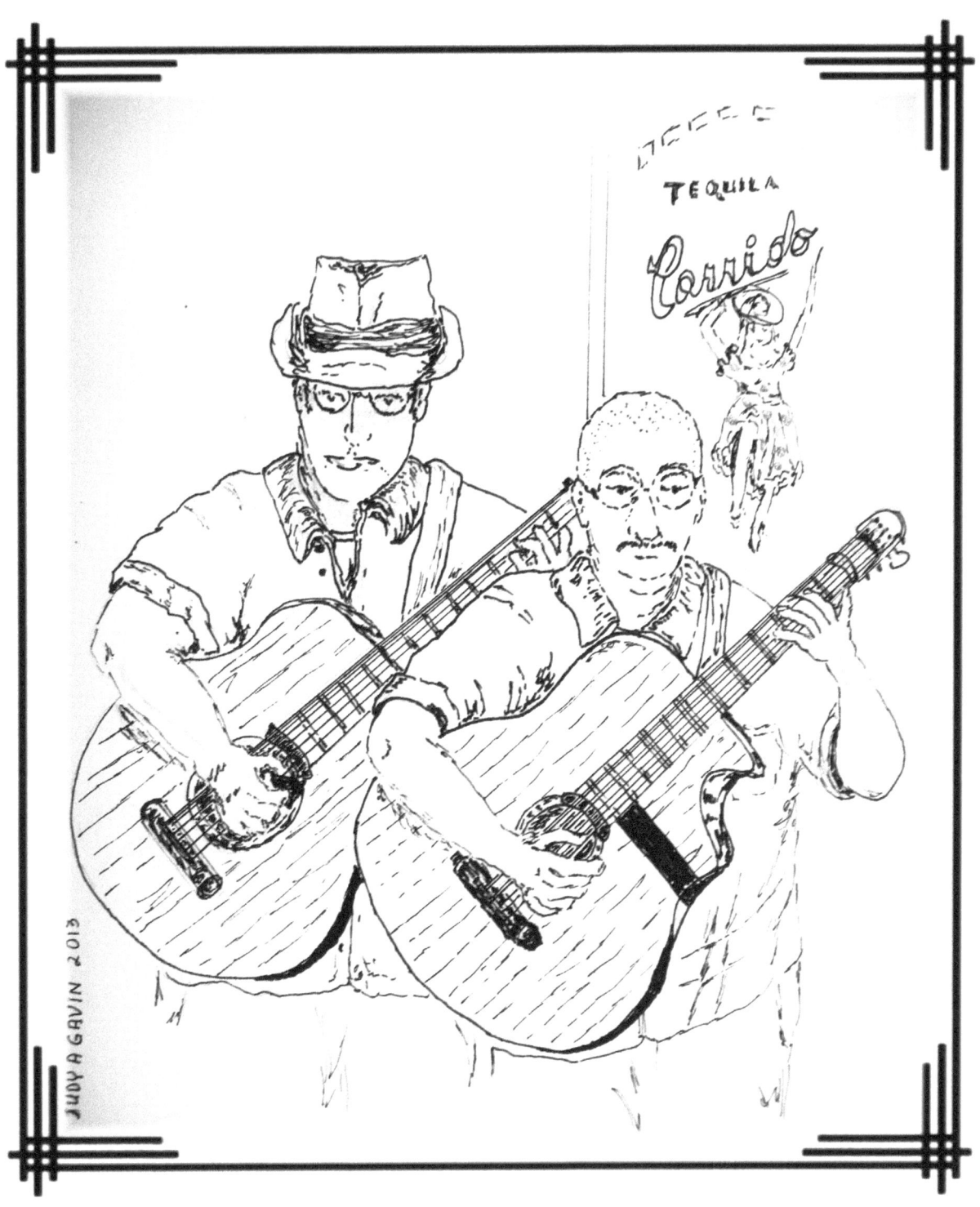

Sketched By: Judith A. Gavin-Holton [summer] 2014

Chapter 11 – KITTY, KITE AND A BOY

This young boy is trying desperately to recover his little brother's kite that was blown by the wind into the bushes outside his grandparent's home. In point of fact, we were trying to make a winning photograph for a township photo contest and this is an ink drawing from our endeavors.

We did have "winning fun" and he was able to retrieve the kite with a few minor tears. His brother got to fly the kite a few more times that day, wind and all.

During this venture their kitty-cat kept trying to be petted by brushing against his legs for attention. The kitty never gave up and followed him around until he bent over and stroked her fur.

The wind can be quite tricky…especially with kites, little boys and a kitty.

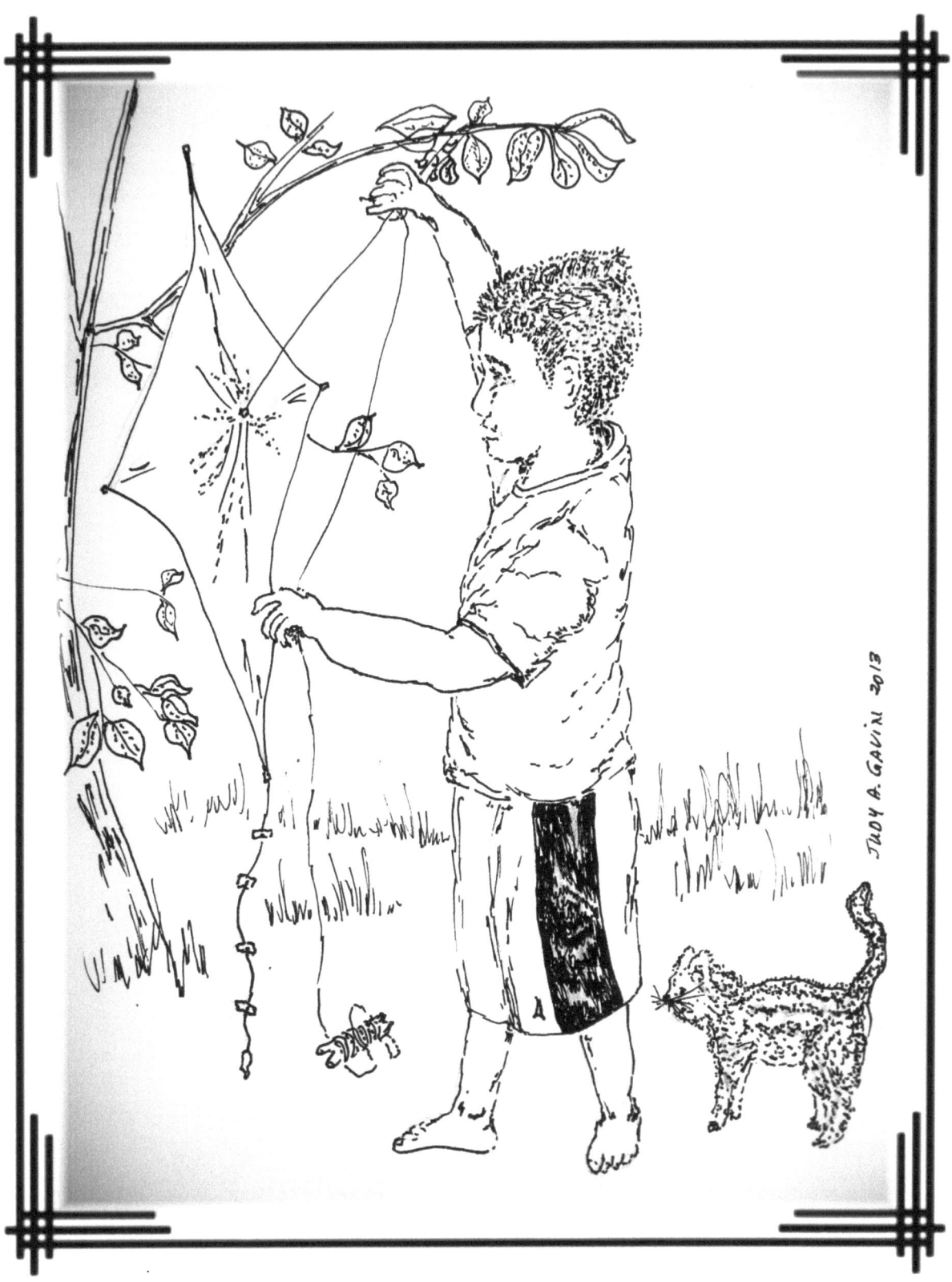

Sketched By: Judith A. Gavin-Holton [summer] 2013

Chapter 12 – MY AUNT RUTH

My Aunt Ruth was a tiny toddler all of two and a half years old sitting in front of her grandmother's house in the state of Florida. She was sitting in a wicker chair holding her treasured dolly and looking for her dress-up hat which had fallen to the porch boards. The chair is small because her grandmother was a small person.

My Aunt Ruth was born with blonde hair and it remained blonde her whole life, passing on at the ripe old age of 76 years old in Buffalo, New York. She was always considered to be the "beautiful child" way into adulthood. She used to love chewing gum and snapping it playfully. She had a magnificent laugh that would make any and all smile.

She loved life and it loved her back. "Each day was a fun day" her whole life and she never saw a challenge as serious, only that someone would have to take care of it somehow-someway.

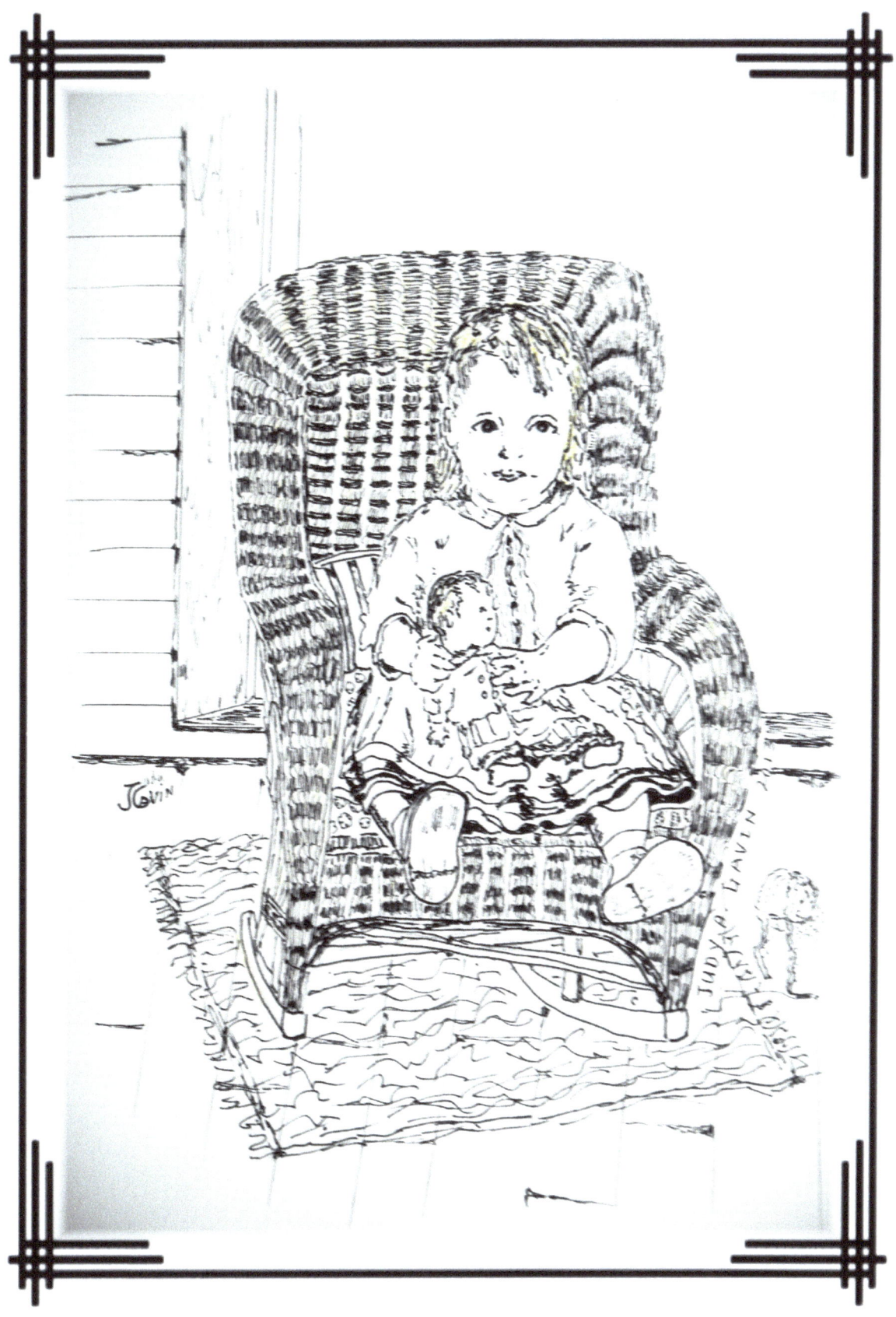

Sketched By: Judith A. Gavin-Holton [summer] 2014

Chapter 13 – BOYS AND TOYS

My niece does Gymkhana, an equestrian event consisting of speed pattern racing and timed games for riders on horses. Timed-speed events such as barrel racing, keyhole race, keg race (also known as "down and back"), flag race, and pole bending are completed. All of these events are designed to display precise, controlled actions and tight teamwork between horse and rider at various speeds. During the summer of 2014, I was able to attend several of her functions and watched her do very well. She loves this sport and handles horses very well.

At one such Gymkhana event, the horses and riders had completed all the races and were being unsaddled for trailer-traveling. My sister and I watched as they strode past us for the day's end.

It was afternoon and going in the opposite direction was a tall lady slowly walking with her horse in tow. Right behind her were two young barefooted boys carrying their sneakers. Right behind them was a small black and white dog on a loose leash.

As we looked up at the horse as he passed us, we noticed what was hanging from the saddle and chuckled. There were at least 3 toy dump trucks and a trailer of sorts hanging from several ropes attached to the horse's saddle horn. They were just walking by without a care in the world and doing their own thing. As we chuckled, I told sister it was a site to be sketched.

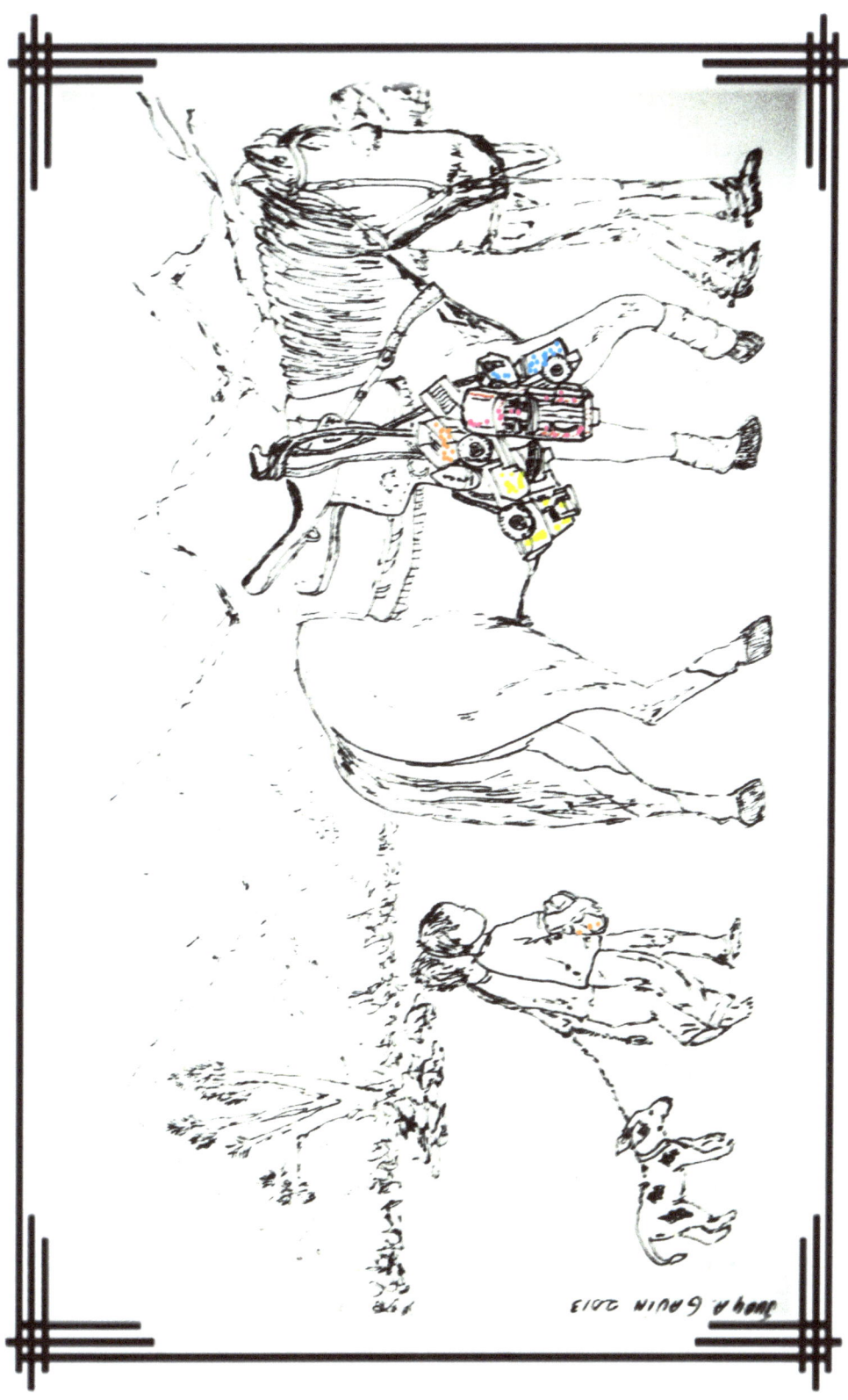

Sketched By: Judith A. Gavin-Holton [fall] 2014

31

Chapter 14 – REMEMBERING AS A TODDLER

I sketched this from an old, old photo so that if it faded anymore, I would still have the loving content expressed with my Mom, my brother and myself being held. We lived on the east side of Buffalo in a first floor duplex rental. It had a neat side yard off to the left of the house, if one was facing it, with a double front gate that we could not open as children.

Mom, every summer while living there, tried her hand at gardening by growing different flowers. One type would die off and another would bloom. She would grumble more or less daily over the constant weed challenges. It rained quite often and some of the flowers would just bend right over and kiss the ground they came from while others bloomed.

Mom always called Lillian, our next door neighbor, to come see the bright new ones and then stand there—as if more were about to pop up from the empty spots yet to start. This was a fun time because Mom was happiest playing in her garden. I never knew why she did not grow vegetables until I was older. She said that nasty critters would come and eat what wasn't theirs' and leave us nothing but useless insect ridden trash with bite marks. She had experienced this as a child when her mom grew needed vegetables.

My grandparents grew everything they could and; yes the critters did come. Grandma would have to throw many apples, pears, carrots, beets, and other vegetables and fruit away because they were half eaten and more, thus contaminated. They had no backyard so grandma planted every kind of fruit and vegetables she could in the front yard. One could barely see the house through the orchard of the front. She used string and wire to hold up the vegetable vines.

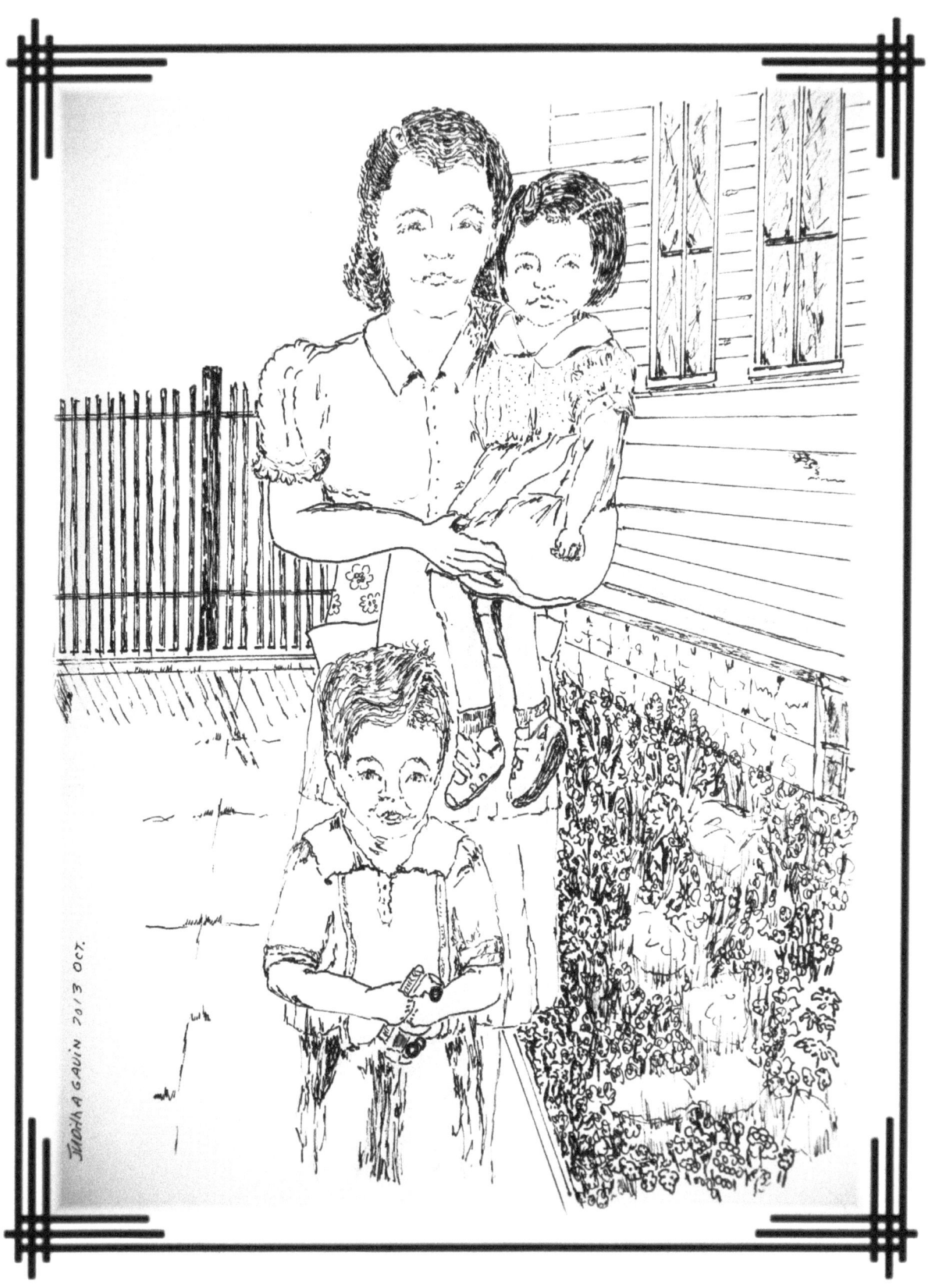

Sketched By: Judith A. Gavin-Holton [early summer] 2014

My mom and Aunty would go over and help Grandma harvest the vegetables and fruits as each type became ready. Once harvested, they would begin the long process of cooking, canning, labeling, storing and sharing. They were for use during the winter into the spring months.

They would listen to the radio for music, *Beulah* stories (read by *Lillian Randolph*), and news while completing their task of canning. They always told many long stories while they canned and I am not sure how many were valid…but they laughed a lot even to tears. We always went home with jars of everything to be placed in our cellar.

www.ingramcontent.com/pod-product-compliance
Lightning Source LLC
Chambersburg PA
CBHW050354180526
45159CB00005B/2018